*P*resented by: _____

*T*o: _____

*F*rom: _____

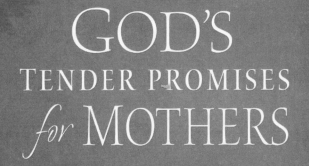

GOD'S
TENDER PROMISES
for MOTHERS

GOD'S
TENDER PROMISES
for MOTHERS

$\mathscr{G}$od is truly amazing. He chooses
to sit with us in the kitchen of life
rather than in the parlor, because He wants
to know us from the inside out.

. . . . $\approx$ . . . .

*For the Son of Man has come to seek
and to save that which was lost.*
LUKE 19:10

Come out from under the covers.
God has chased away the dream monsters
from the closets of your life.

. . . . ∽ . . . .

The LORD is my light and my salvation;
whom shall I fear? The LORD is the strength
of my life; of whom shall I be afraid?

PSALM 27:1

*A*n apple will always be an apple and never an orange. Only you, mother— God's special creature—are given the chance to change your soul.

. . . . ∾ . . . .

For God so loved the world,
that He gave His only begotten Son,
that whoever believes in Him
should not perish but have everlasting life.
JOHN 3:16

*H*uman sweat never made a rainbow.
When you think seriously about it,
it makes little sense to try to impress God.

· · · · ❧ · · · ·

For by grace you have been saved through faith,
and that not of yourselves; it is the gift of God,
not of works, lest anyone should boast.
Ephesians 2:8–9

$\mathcal{G}$od is many things to you, Mother:
a caring Father, One who believes in you
even more than you believe in yourself,
the Giver of life everlasting.

· · · · ❧ · · · ·

Most assuredly, I say to you,
he who believes in Me has everlasting life.
JOHN 6:47

*M*others know: That which you
give freely to others will be given
back to you in greater measure.
It's a rule of God's kingdom!

. . . . ∾ . . . .

Give, and it will be given to you: good measure,
pressed down, shaken together, and running over
will be put into your bosom. For with the same measure
that you use, it will be measured back to you.

LUKE 6:38

Mother always said that even the
youngest child can reach up
and grasp the loving hand of God.

. . . . ∾ . . . .

I love those who love me,
and those who seek me diligently will find me.
PROVERBS 8:17

$\mathscr{C}$ommitment to God means
believing He is who He says He is,
and acting on that faith as you strive
to be a godly mother.

· · · · ∾ · · · ·

Whoever confesses that Jesus is the Son of God,
God abides in him, and he in God.
1 John 4:15

$\mathcal{M}$other, you need never settle for rags
when God promises to give you
new garments.

· · · · ∾ · · · ·

Therefore, if anyone is in Christ,
he is a new creation;
old things have passed away;
behold all things have become new.
2 CORINTHIANS 5:17

9

Mother taught us that our heavenly Father sees the transgressions in the shadows as easily as those on the mountaintop. The good news is that He forgives both equally.

. . . . ∼ . . . .

*If we confess our sins. He is faithful and just
to forgive us our sins and to cleanse us
from all unrighteousness.*
1 JOHN 1:9

*G*od never remembers a
wrong that is confessed. Put your
sins behind you—by putting
God before you.

. . . . ∼ . . . .

I, even I, am He who blots out
your transgressions for My own sake;
and I will not remember your sins.
ISAIAH 43:25

$\mathcal{G}$od's truth can break the shackles
that bind the most desperate person.
It sets us free from all that imprisons us.

· · · · ~ · · · ·

And you shall know the truth,
and the truth shall make you free.
JOHN 8:32

*C*hrist turns a crust of bread into
a banquet; with Him mere existence
becomes life everlasting.

· · · · ∾ · · · ·

Most assuredly, I say to you, he who hears My word
and believes in Him who sent Me has everlasting life,
and shall not come into judgment,
but has passed from death into life.

JOHN 5:24

*M*other, I want you to know that
Jesus is the password to a better life.

. . . . ~ . . . .

He who believes and is baptized will be saved.

MARK 16:16

You only value Jesus at all
when you value Him above all.

. . . . ❧ . . . .

But if we walk in the light as He is in the light,
we have fellowship with one another, and the blood
of Jesus Christ His Son cleanses us from all sin.

1 JOHN 1:7

*T*hank you, Mother, for teaching me
to trust the all-seeing eyes of God
to help me in every area of my life.

. . . . ❧ . . . .

For the eyes of the LORD run to and fro
throughout the whole earth, to show Himself
strong on behalf of those whose heart is loyal to Him.
2 CHRONICLES 16:9

$\mathcal{D}$on't forget, Mother, you are
never a number with God.
With Him, you are always
at the head of the line.

. . . . ∾ . . . .

Then the King will say to those on His right hand,
"Come, you blessed of My Father, inherit the kingdom
prepared for you from the foundation of the world."

$\mathcal{T}$o all busy mothers: God wants
to be your first choice,
not your last resort.

. . . . ∾ . . . .

All that the Father gives Me will come to Me,
and the one who comes to Me
I will by no means cast out.
JOHN 6:37

A dewdrop acts out the will of God
as surely as the thunderstorm.
God cares little about size;
He cares immensely about service.

. . . . ∾ . . . .

For the mountains shall depart and the hills be removed, but
My kindness shall not depart from you, . . .

ISAIAH 54:10

The tree with deep roots weathers
the hurricane. Establish your roots
deep in God's Word to weather
the storms of life.

. . . . ~ . . . .

All Scripture is given by inspiration of God,
and is profitable for doctrine, for reproof, for correction,
for instruction in righteousness.
2 Timothy 3:16

$\mathcal{G}$od's whisper can be heard
beyond the stars and beneath the seas—
but listen, Mother, and you will hear
His voice echo in your heart.

. . . . ∼ . . . .

*Then you will call upon Me and go
and pray to Me, and I will listen to you.
And you will seek Me and find Me, when
you search for Me with all your heart.*
JEREMIAH 29:12-13

*F*aith is a laboratory course,
not a lecture. Put the Bible to the test
and watch God at work in your efforts
to be a godly mother.

· · · · ⚬ · · · ·

For the word of God is living and powerful,
and sharper than any two-edged sword, piercing
even to the division of soul and spirit, and of joints
and marrow, and is a discerner of the thoughts
and intents of the heart.

HEBREWS 4:12

*I*n a world of bravado and compromise,
the Word of God is an oasis
of sanity and joy for mothers.

· · · · 〜 · · · ·

Every word of God is pure; He is a shield
to those who put their trust in Him.
PROVERBS 30:5

To find true security, accept God's
peace—to know great freedom,
accept His mercy and love.

. . . . ❧ . . . .

Heaven and earth shall pass away,
but My words will by no means pass away.
MARK 13:31

The only crutches on the King's highway are those tossed away by the side of the road. Mother, you can walk today in God's wholeness.

. . . . ✍ . . . .

The steps of a good man are ordered by the LORD:
and He delights in his way.
PSALM 37:23

$\mathscr{I}$n a world where blind guides
lead the unsuspecting to oblivion,
God promises to give both sight and insight
to dads and moms who must
guide their families.

· · · · ∾ · · · ·

*I will instruct you and teach you in the way
you should go; I will guide you with My eye.*

$\mathcal{T}$hank you for teaching me, Mother,
that life with God is endless hope—
without Him it is a hopeless end.

. . . . ❧ . . . .

But you are a chosen generation, a royal priesthood,
a holy nation, His own special people.
1 PETER 2:9

If you are looking for direction, Mother, seek God's face. If you would have life abundant, obey His words.

. . . . ⁓ . . . .

Give attention to my words; incline your ear to my sayings. Do not let them depart from your eyes; keep them in the midst of your heart; for they are life to those who find them, and health to all their flesh.

PROVERBS 4:20‑22

$\mathscr{G}$ood news, Mom! With God,
your line of credit
has no limit.

. . . . ~ . . . .

*And my God shall supply all your need
according to His riches in glory by Christ Jesus.*

PHILIPPIANS 4:19

$\mathscr{F}$aith provides a soft pillow
for weary worriers—especially mothers.
Leave your cares in the hands of God.

· · · · ∼ · · · ·

*If you keep My commandments, you will abide
in My love, just as I have kept My Father's
commandments and abide in His love.*

JOHN 15:7

The crown you will wear in heaven
one day is being fashioned on earth today.
Your crown will be beautiful, Mother.

. . . . ∾ . . . .

Bless the LORD, O my soul, and forget not
all His benefits; who forgives all your iniquities,
who heals all your diseases, who redeems your
life from destruction, who crowns you with
lovingkindness and tender mercies.

PSALM 103:2-4

$\mathcal{M}$others know well that
you will always find yourself by losing
yourself in the lives of others.

. . . . 〜 . . . .

And God is able to make all grace abound
toward you that you, always having all sufficiency
in all things, may have an abundance for every good work.
2 CORINTHIANS 9:8

$\mathcal{J}$esus is the bread that is never stale;
He is the water that is forever pure.

· · · · ∾ · · · ·

And Jesus said to them, "I am the bread of life.
He who comes to Me shall never hunger,
and he who believes in Me shall never thirst."

John 6:35

*G*od's answer is in your every question.
Through His power and might
He fulfills all your needs.

· · · · ~ · · · ·

*But those who wait on the LORD shall renew
their strength; they shall mount up with wings
like eagles, they shall run and not be weary,
they shall walk and not faint.*
ISAIAH 40:31

$\mathcal{D}$on't forget, Mother—worry shatters
the peace of life. Faith puts things
back together.

. . . . ❧ . . . .

Peace I leave with you, My peace I give to you;
not as the world gives do I give to you.
Let not your heart be troubled, neither let it be afraid.
JOHN 14:27

$\mathcal{G}$od gathers the remnants of a mother's
life and weaves them into a work
of dignity and purpose.

. . . . ~ . . . .

*Being confident of this very thing, that He
who has begun a good work in you will
complete it until the day of Jesus Christ.*

PHILIPPIANS 1:6

$\mathscr{B}$efore you face the challenges
of your day, Mother, face the day with
God—He will help you to
meet those challenges.

. . . . ❧ . . . .

He who dwells in the secret place of the Most High
shall abide under the shadow of the Almighty.
I will say of the LORD, He is my refuge and
my fortress; my God, in Him I will trust.
PSALM 91:1-2

*K*eeping in shape is great,
but soul-building requires much
more discipline than body-building.
Choose the trainer of your spirit well.

· · · · ~ · · · ·

Fear not, for I am with you; be not dismayed,
for I am your God. I will strengthen you, yes,
I will help you, I will uphold you
with My righteous right hand.

ISAIAH 41:10

$\mathcal{T}$he sky never falls no matter
how hard it rains. God's love for you,
Mother, never fails, regardless of your pain.

. . . . ∾ . . . .

Be strong and of good courage, do not fear
nor be afraid of them; for the LORD *your God,*
He is the One who goes with you.
He will not leave you nor forsake you.

DEUTERONOMY 31:6

*S*peak kind words,
and you will hear kind echoes.
Thanks for all the kind echoes, Mom.

. . . . ∼ . . . .

Pleasant words are like a honeycomb,
sweetness to the soul and health to the bones.
PROVERBS 16:24

*M*other, when you feel your life has
become a silent cocoon, be encouraged.
Before long, you will emerge from
your quietness and become
God's person of beauty.

· · · · ≈ · · · ·

Heal me, O LORD, and I shall be healed;
save me, and I shall be saved, for You are my praise.
JEREMIAH 17:14

Mother always said:
"A gift is not a gift unless you give it
with your heart."

. . . . ~ . . . .

Give, and it will be given to you: good measure,
pressed down, shaken together, and running over,
will be put into your bosom. For with the same
measure that you use, it will be measured back to you.

LUKE 6:38

$\mathcal{L}$ook for the face of God in the winter
of discontent as well as in the summer
of joy. He is the God for all seasons.

· · · · ❧ · · · ·

To everything there is a season, a time
for every purpose under heaven.
ECCLESIASTES 3:1

A prism has no life in the dark;
only in the richness of sunlight
will it sparkle. Keep your faith
in the light and see it shine.

. . . . ∽ . . . .

Delight yourself also in the Lord; and He
shall give you the desires of your heart.
Psalm 37:4

44

Mother, if you brood
over your troubles, you will
hatch despair. Trust them to God,
and your victory is sure.

. . . . ❧ . . . .

Trust in the LORD with all your heart, and lean
not on your own understanding; in all your ways
acknowledge Him, and He shall direct your paths.
PROVERBS 3:5-6

45

A mother's motto:

It is better to wear out doing good

than to rust out doing little or nothing.

. . . . ～ . . . .

I will instruct you and teach you in the way you
should go; I will guide you with My eye.

PSALM 32:8

*W*ithout a foundation, even castles
are little more than piles of stones.
Stability and structure come
before elegance and beauty.

. . . . ∾ . . . .

*But the Lord is faithful, who will establish you
and guard you from the evil one.*
2 THESSALONIANS 3:3

47

$\mathcal{L}$ove is its own reward; hate is its own punishment. The surest way to get rid of an enemy is to make that person your friend.

. . . . ❧ . . . .

Since you have purified your souls in obeying the truth through the Spirit in sincere love of the brethren, love one another fervently with a pure heart.
1 PETER 1:22

A note on Mother's refrigerator:
God wants to be more than a 911
number. Call on him at all times . . .
not just in a crisis.

. . . . ≈ . . . .

He shall call upon Me, and I will answer him;
I will be with him in trouble;
I will deliver him and honor him.
Psalm 91:15

$\mathcal{I}$can still hear my mother's
words of wisdom. "You can run, but you
cannot hide. God's unfailing love
will seek you out and find you."

· · · · ≈ · · · ·

He will not forsake you nor destroy you,
nor forget the covenant of your fathers
which He swore to them.
DEUTERONOMY 4:31

*S*he stands firmest
who kneels soonest. Take your concerns
to God, Mother. He waits patiently
to supply your every need.

. . . . ≈ . . . .

Cast your burden on the LORD, and He
shall sustain you; He shall never permit
the righteous to be moved.
PSALM 55:22

$\mathcal{Y}$ou have to pass by the thorns to get
to the rose. So when you prick yourself,
remember, you are on the path
to fragrance and beauty.

. . . . ∾ . . . .

*And we know that all things work together for good
to those who love God, to those who are the called
according to His purpose.*

ROMANS 8:28

$\mathcal{M}$others, teach your children
to be quick in what they stand for
and slow in what they fall for.

. . . . ❧ . . . .

For we have become partakers of Christ
if we hold the beginning of our
confidence steadfast to the end.
HEBREWS 3:14

A newborn chick doesn't know it's alive until its world begins to crumble. What seems like the collapse of your universe may be just an exciting beginning.

· · · · ⌒ · · · ·

Now faith is the substance of things hoped for,
the evidence of things not seen.

HEBREWS 11:1

*F*ool's gold might catch your eye,
but God's gold—truth, mercy, and love—
will capture your heart.

. . . . ∼ . . . .

But without faith it is impossible to please Him
for he who comes to God must believe that
He is, and that He is a rewarder of those
who diligently seek Him.

HEBREWS 11:6

$\mathcal{A}$ truth my mother always taught:
The oil of courtesy smoothes away friction.
When in doubt about whether to apologize
or not—apologize. The smallest act of
kindness can save a friendship.

. . . . ∾ . . . .

Beloved, let us love one another, for love is of God; and
everyone who loves is born of God and knows God.
He who does not love does not know God,
for God is love.
1 JOHN 4:7-8

Even mothers sometimes need
to color outside the lines of life to add
more shades of beauty. Live life
with God in creativity and joy.

. . . . ～ . . . .

Abide in Me, and I in you. As the branch
cannot bear fruit of itself, unless it abides in the
vine, neither can you, unless you abide in Me.
JOHN 15:4

If you remain wrapped up
in yourself, you may discover a very small
package. Give yourself away—let God's
love make you all He created you to be.

· · · · ☙ · · · ·

A new commandment I give to you, that you love
one another; as I have loved you, that you also love
one another. By this all will know that you are
My disciples, if you have love for one another.

JOHN 13:34–35

58

Eternity is a short time to spend with God—it is an endless destiny of pain and despair without Him.

· · · · ∿ · · · ·

Jesus said to her, "I am the resurrection and the life. He who believes in Me, though he may die, he shall live. And whoever lives and believes in Me shall never die."

JOHN 11:25–26

$\mathcal{L}$ike a mother humming a lullabye,
God sings to His children—
listen for the songs of God in the night.
Let them give you rest and sleep.

. . . . $\approx$ . . . .

My sheep hear My voice, and I know them,
and they follow Me. And I give them eternal life,
and they shall never perish; neither shall
anyone snatch them out of My hand.
JOHN 10:27-28

Some people wait for the
hearse to take them to church—
by then it's too late!

. . . . ∾ . . . .

I must work the works of Him who sent Me
while it is day; the night is coming
when no one can work.
JOHN 9:4

*R*emember, Mother,
that worry makes mountains out
of molehills. God makes molehills
out of mountains.

. . . . ❧ . . . .

Great is the LORD, and greatly to be praised
in the city of our God, in His holy mountain.
PSALM 48:1

$\mathcal{G}$od knocks at your door, Mother,
but He will never knock down
your door. Listen for His gentle knock.
Accept Him as your friend.

. . . . ~ . . . .

Behold, I stand at the door and knock. If anyone
hears My voice and opens the door, I will come in
to him and dine with him, and he with Me.

REVELATION 3:20

The journey to God starts with one small step. After that it's one step at a time. He doesn't expect us to run the mile—but He promises to give us strength to live each day for Him.

. . . . ⌢ . . . .

Walk in all the ways that I have commanded you, that it may be well with you.
JEREMIAH 7:23

Some people only know how to make a living. With God as your Father, you can know how to make a *life*.

. . . . ∼ . . . .

If you love Me, keep my commandments.
He who has My commandments and keeps them,
it is he who loves Me.

JOHN 14:15

Mother, you always said,
"You can never judge a gift by its
wrappings." Likewise, you will never know
God's great gift until you open
your heart to Him.

. . . . ～ . . . .

The LORD will give grace and glory; no good thing
will He withhold from those who walk uprightly.
PSALM 84:11

Even a bee can be too busy
making honey to savor the taste.
Mother, why not spend time
today enjoying your heavenly Father.

. . . . ～ . . . .

For whoever finds me finds life,
and obtains favor from the LORD.
PROVERBS 8:35

Some Christians journey barefoot, others with designer shoes. The truth is, it's not the shoes on the feet that count, but the feet in the shoes.
You have beautiful feet, Mother.

· · · · ～ · · · ·

But now God has set the members,
each one of them, in the body just as He pleased.
1 CORINTHIANS 12:18

*G*od doesn't scold us
for asking too much of Him,
only for asking too little.

. . . . ∼ . . . .

*If you then, being evil, know how to give good gifts
to your children, how much more will your
heavenly Father give the Holy Spirit
to those who ask Him!*

LUKE 11:13

A note on Mother's refrigerator:
God promises to give us our daily
bread. He doesn't guarantee
it will be buttered.

. . . . ~ . . . .

Behold, I am with you and will keep you
wherever you go, and will bring you back
to this land; for I will not leave you until I have
done what I have spoken to you.
GENESIS 28:15

Mother, a mirror and a window
are both made of glass: One shows
you yourself, the other shows you
the world. Let God give you His
perspective on the difference.

. . . . ∼ . . . .

*Now we see in a mirror, dimly, but then
face to face . . . now abide faith, hope, love . . .
but the greatest of these is love.*
1 CORINTHIANS 13:13

A flood begins with a drop of rain. A habit of sin begins with an act of sin. Choose your habits well. They will either become your power or your prison.

· · · · ∽ · · · ·

No temptation has overtaken you except such as is common to man; but God is faithful, who will not allow you to be tempted beyond what you are able, but with the temptation will also make the way of escape, that you may be able to bear it.

1 Corinthians 10:13

There is more power in the open
hand than in the clenched fist.
Thank you for your open hand
of love and kindness.

. . . . ∾ . . . .

And we urge you, brethren . . . to esteem them
very highly in love for their work's sake.
Be at peace among yourselves.
1 THESSALONIANS 5:12–13

A hundred voices can produce a beautiful melody or an irksome cacophony—it all depends on how well they follow directions.

. . . . ∾ . . . .

Behold how good and how pleasant it is
for brethren to dwell together in unity!
<small>PSALM</small> 133:1

Mother always said that the
largest room in the world
is the room for improvement.

· · · · ∾ · · · ·

And that you, always having all sufficiency
in all things, may have an abundance
for every good work.
2 CORINTHIANS 9:8

We hear God well when
we listen to Him often. Pray
without ceasing. Make every moment
one of praise to the Father.

. . . . ∾ . . . .

And all these blessings shall come upon you
and overtake you, because you obey
the voice of the LORD your God.

DEUTERONOMY 28:2

$\mathcal{M}$other, you can know your heart

by what pleases your spirit.

May it be obedience to God,

who gives all good gifts.

. . . . ❧ . . . .

If they obey and serve Him, they shall spend their days

in prosperity, and their years in pleasures.

JOB 36:11

One of Mother's favorite mottos:
"Satan is never content with a nibble
of your soul. He wants to devour it
completely. Be wary of his tactics."

· · · · ❧ · · · ·

Be sober, be vigilant; because your adversary
the devil walks about like a roaring lion,
seeking whom he may devour.
1 PETER 5:8

A note from Mother:
If you feel you have no faults,
rest assured you have at least one.
Pride is the devil's hook, and
he knows how to use it well.

. . . . ❧ . . . .

*Therefore submit to God. Resist the devil
and he will flee from you.*
JAMES 4:7

*A*en't you glad there are
no renters in heaven?
God gives the deed outright,
or He doesn't give it at all.

· · · · ∽ · · · ·

In My Father's house are many mansions;
if it were not so, I would have told you. I go
to prepare a place for you. And if I go and prepare
a place for you, I will come again and receive you
to Myself; that where I am, there you may be also.
JOHN 14:2–3

$\mathcal{T}$he devil wins few converts
on deathbeds.

. . . . ∾ . . . .

For the wages of sin is death, but the gift of God
is eternal life in Christ Jesus our Lord.

ROMANS 6:23

$\mathcal{M}$ost people have heard "no"
all their lives. What a privilege to say "yes"
to them in the name of Jesus.

. . . . ∾ . . . .

For God did not send His Son into the world
to condemn the world, but that the world
through Him might be saved.
JOHN 3:17

If you are only a self-made mother, your foundation is poorly laid. Let God strengthen your structure through His wisdom and might.

. . . . ❧ . . . .

Commit your works to the LORD, and your thoughts will be established.
<small>PROVERBS 16:3</small>

A bowl of soup eaten with
God's blessing is more satisfying
than a banquet without it. Meals with you,
Mother, are always a banquet.

· · · · ～ · · · ·

I have been young, and now am old;
yet I have not seen the righteous forsaken,
nor his descendants begging bread.
PSALM 37:25

*M*other always said:
"The secret of contentment lies
not in possessing many things,
but in wanting few things."

. . . . ∿ . . . .

The LORD will guide you continually, and
satisfy your soul in drought, and strengthen
your bones; you shall be like a watered garden,
and like a spring of water, whose waters do not fall.

ISAIAH 58:11

$\mathcal{S}$ome people face a closed door
and see only an impediment. Why not
knock on the door and believe God's
promise that it will open to love and hope?

. . . . ❧ . . . .

Ask, and it will be given to you; seek, and you
will find; knock, and it will be opened to you.
For everyone who asks receives, and he who seeks
finds, and to him who knocks it will be opened.
MATTHEW 7:7–8

*N*ever forget, Mother,
that God knows you, loves you,
and recognizes you even without
a name tag.

. . . . ◇ . . . .

You are worthy, O Lord, to receive glory and
honor and power; for You created all things,
and by Your will they exist and were created.
REVELATION 4:11

A note from Mother:
God promises to take care of
the needy, not the greedy.

· · · · ∾ · · · ·

Let us therefore come boldly to the throne of grace,
that we may obtain mercy and find grace
to help in time of need.

HEBREWS 4:16

$\mathscr{T}$o live a good life, you need
to be a good person. To live a great life,
you must serve a great God.
Mother, your life has been good and great!

· · · · ✎ · · · ·

Call to Me, and I will answer you, and show you
great and mighty things, which you do not know.

JEREMIAH 33:3

$\mathcal{T}$he secret to being a
generous Christian in public is
being a committed disciple in secret.
You have been as generous in secret
as in public, Mother.

. . . . ≈ . . . .

But you, when you pray, go into your room, and
when you have shut your door, pray to your
Father who is in the secret place; and your Father
who sees in secret will reward you openly.

MATTHEW 6:6

Mother always said that
when you stand for nothing, you
are apt to fall for anything. She taught us
to stand firm in the knowledge
of God's love.

. . . . ⮂ . . . .

The Lord is not slack concerning His promise,
as some count slackness, but is longsuffering
toward us, not willing that any should perish
but that all should come to repentance.

2 PETER 3:9

When you earn the wages of sin, you are grossly underpaid. The devil is a devious employer who promises much and delivers little.

· · · · ∼ · · · ·

Who among you fears the LORD? Who obeys the voice of His Servant? Who walks in darkness and has no light? Let him trust in the name of the LORD and rely upon his God.

ISAIAH 50:10

$\mathcal{S}$ome people settle for a god they can turn off and on at will. You will know God is real when you realize he will never leave you nor forsake you. He is your eternal light.

· · · · ◁ · · · ·

He himself has said, "I will never leave you
nor forsake you."
HEBREWS 13:5

A note on Mother's refrigerator:
An untended leak can sink a ship,
and unresolved anger can destroy a
friendship. Fix the leak.

. . . . ⁓ . . . .

Let all bitterness, wrath, anger, clamor, and evil
speaking be put away from you, with all malice.
And be kind to one another, tenderhearted, forgiving
one another, even as God in Christ forgave you.
EPHESIANS 4:31–32

Mother, without God's mercy
and comfort, you will remain lost at sea—
unsure of your direction and with little
hope of finding port.

· · · · ⤳ · · · ·

The LORD your God in your midst, the Mighty One,
will save; He will rejoice over you with gladness.
ZEPHANIAH 3:17

Even a turtle must stick out its neck
if it wants to move ahead. God will show
you the general direction you must travel,
but the specifics of the journey are up to you.
Thank you for encouraging me
to stick my neck out, Mom.

. . . . ∼ . . . .

*Thus says the LORD, your Redeemer,
the Holy One of Israel: I am the LORD your God,
who teaches you to profit, who leads you
by the way you should go.*
ISAIAH 48:17

Some people use the church like a refrigerator: to preserve themselves as they already are. God wants the church to be more like a toaster: heating us up and moving us out into service.

· · · · ❧ · · · ·

Let your light so shine before men, that they may see your good works and glorify your Father in heaven.
MATTHEW 5:16.

$\mathcal{J}$elly beans come in all colors
and flavors—like mothers.
Everyone is a different flavor, because
God made us that way!

. . . . ❧ . . . .

Beloved, if God so loved us, we also
ought to love one another.
1 JOHN 4:11

$\mathcal{T}$hank you for teaching us, Mother,
that God never makes deals. That's the
devil's tactic. If what Satan promises
seems too good to be true,
you can rest assured it is!

. . . . ∿ . . . .

*For I am persuaded that neither death nor life,
nor angels nor principalities nor powers, nor things
present nor things to come, nor height nor depth,
nor any other created thing, shall be able to separate us
from the love of God which is in Christ Jesus our Lord.*

ROMANS 8:38–39

$\mathcal{M}$ary gave birth to a king,
but didn't complain that no one
had made reservations for her at
the inn. Serving God means serving
Him without guarantees—regardless.

. . . . ≈ . . . .

He said to them, "Whoever desires to come
after Me, let him deny himself, and
take up his cross, and follow Me."

MARK 8:34

$\mathcal{S}$leep is God's way of saying,
"Trust Me." Trust Him today. He will
never let you down, Mother, whether
you are awake or asleep.

· · · · ≈ · · · ·

I will both lie down in peace, and sleep;
for You alone, O LORD, make me dwell in safety.
PSALM 4:8

A dandelion blossom must
fade and die for the seed to spread.
The life that appears too perfect
often has few seeds to share.

. . . . ∼ . . . .

Most assuredly, I say to you, unless a grain of
wheat falls into the ground and dies, it remains alone;
but if it dies, it produces much grain. He who loves
his life will lose it, and he who hates his life
in this world will keep it for eternal life.
JOHN 12:24-25

At an appointed time
in divine history God carved His laws
on stone tablets. Today, He carves
them deep within our hearts.

· · · · ❧ · · · ·

Your word I have hidden in my heart,
that I might not sin against You.
PSALM 119:11

Never forget to immerse yourself
in God's holy Word, Mother.
He will make something
wonderful of your life.

· · · · ∼ · · · ·

The counsel of the LORD stands forever,
the plans of His heart to all generations.
PSALM 33:11

Mothers are like flowers.
Some grow best in the sun;
others do well in the shade.
God plants us where we grow best.

. . . . ～ . . . .

*But let all those rejoice who put their trust
in You; let them ever shout for joy, because
You defend them; let those also who love
Your name be joyful in You.*

PSALM 5:11

God plays favorites—with everyone.
His heart is big enough to love you
more than you can love yourself.

. . . . ≈ . . . .

We love Him because He first loved us.
1 JOHN 4:19

You are one of God's greatest risks.
He paid dearly for you without warranty,
money-back guarantee, or thirty-day
return policy. Yet, he loves you and
will never leave you or forsake you.

. . . . ∾ . . . .

For the LORD will not forsake His people,
for His great name's sake, because it has
pleased the LORD to make you His people.
1 SAMUEL 12:22

$\mathcal{M}$other always said that
if you discover you are
full of yourself, you are empty.
When you admit you are empty,
then you will be filled.

· · · · $\approx$ · · · ·

God resists the proud,
but gives grace to the humble.
1 PETER 5:5

It is pointless to appear
to be a godly mother to the world
if you are not loving and kind
in your home.

· · · · ~ · · · ·

He who is slow to anger is better than the mighty,
and he who rules his spirit than he who takes a city.
PROVERBS 16:32

Holding grudges makes a person bitter—not better. Ask God to help you control your spirit, and speak the truth in love.

. . . . ∼ . . . .

Be angry, and do not sin: do not let
the sun go down on your wrath.
EPHESIANS 4:26

A note from Mother:

Even a stamp takes a licking

before it reaches its destination.

Never, never, never give up.

God is on your side.

. . . . ∽ . . . .

In God I have put my trust; I will not be afraid.
What can man do to me?

PSALM 56:11

$\mathcal{P}$eople who disguise their diseases cannot expect to be cured. Seek God's counsel for the challenges of being a mother.

. . . . ~ . . . .

For His anger is but for a moment, His favor
is for life; weeping may endure for a night,
but joy comes in the morning.

PSALM 30:5

A dead fish floats easily downstream, but one that is alive swims against the tide. God expects us to swim upstream.

. . . . ～ . . . .

Be of good courage, and He shall strengthen your heart, all you who hope in the LORD.

PSALM 31:24

When you are worried about
your children, remember:
Worry is like a rocking chair.
You may feel like you're doing something,
but it won't get you anywhere.

. . . . ～ . . . .

It is good that one should hope and
wait quietly for the salvation of the LORD.
LAMENTATIONS 3:26

The only people we
should try to get even with
are those who have been good to us.
I could never get even with you Mother.
You have been too good to me.

· · · · ～ · · · ·

The end of a thing is better than its beginning;
the patient in spirit is better than the proud in spirit.
Do not hasten in your spirit to be angry, for anger
rests in the bosom of fools.
ECCLESIASTES 7:8–9

If God gave us indisputable evidence of His being, we would have no need for faith. Faith is the essence of things we may never see.

· · · · ❧ · · · ·

Knowing that the testing of your faith produces patience. But let patience have its perfect work, that you may be perfect and complete, lacking nothing.

JAMES 1:3–4

Even for mothers, *if* is the largest word in the English language. It reveals the smallness of our faith and the depth of our desires.

. . . . ❧ . . . .

Jesus said to him, "If you can believe,
all things are possible to him who believes."
MARK 9:23

$\mathcal{L}$ike a muscle, faith must be
exercised to be strong. This is the reason
for the challenges in your life.

. . . . ~ . . . .

For whatever is born of God overcomes the world.
And this is the victory that has overcome
the world—our faith.
1 John 5:4

*P*ouring perfume on a pig,
won't make it a lady. Why change your
image unless you first change your life?

. . . . ~ . . . .

He who hears My word and believes in Him
who sent Me has everlasting life, and shall not come
into judgment, but has passed from death into life.

JOHN 5:24

*It's more useful to exercise
your backbone than your jawbone.
In your Christian faith, let your walk
be consistent with your talk.*

. . . . ≈ . . . .

*The LORD knows the days of the upright,
and their inheritance shall be forever.*
PSALM 37:18

$\mathcal{I}$f the road you are walking
is too free from care, check to see
if you are headed in the right direction.
Satan loves to change the road signs.

. . . . ∾ . . . .

*You shall walk after the LORD your God and
fear Him, and keep His commandments and obey
His voice; you shall serve Him and hold fast to Him.*
DEUTERONOMY 13:4

$\mathscr{G}$od's tests are invariably
true or false, not multiple choice.

· · · · ≈ · · · ·

Then Jesus said to him, "Away with you, Satan!
for it is written, You shall worship the LORD your God,
and Him only you shall serve."

MATTHEW 4:10

When you teach your teen-agers
to drive, teach them also that the road
to perdition has many detours
and allows for few U-turns.

. . . . ❦ . . . .

*The Lord knows how to deliver
the godly out of temptations.*
2 PETER 2:9

$\mathcal{O}$nly God's Word ends with the
ultimate "happily ever after"—but with God
it's not just the end of the story.

· · · · ❧ · · · ·

*And this is the testimony: that God has given
us eternal life, and this life is in His Son.*
1 John 5:11

No one can build ultimate
security on things or people. Real
strength comes from relying on God.

. . . . ≈ . . . .

I can do all things through Christ
who strengthens me.
PHILIPPIANS 4:13

*A*dvice from Mother:

If you enter into an agreement
with the devil, read the fine print. The down
payment for sin may be small, but the regular
installments stretch through eternity.

· · · · ∾ · · · ·

Blessed is the man who endures
temptation; for when he has been approved, he
will receive the crown of life which the LORD has
promised to those who love Him.

ISAIAH 26:3

$\mathscr{R}$emember, Mother,
on the road to heaven, you
never travel alone. God and His people
are your constant companions.

. . . . $\approx$ . . . .

Finally, brethren, farewell. Become complete.
Be of good comfort, be of one mind, live in peace;
and the God of love and peace will be with you.
2 CORINTHIANS 13:11

The devil is a good salesman,
but a miserable traveling companion.
He is a pest and a bore, and never pays
his share of the fare.

. . . . ❧ . . . .

Thus says the LORD: Stand in the ways and see,
and ask for the old paths, where the good way is, and
walk in it; then you will find rest for your souls.
JEREMIAH 6:16

$\mathscr{F}$aith is never graded on a curve—
you simply pass or fail. Let your faith grow.

. . . . ∾ . . . .

He did not waver at the promise of God
through unbelief, but was strengthened in faith,
giving glory to God, and being fully convinced that what
He had promised He was also able to perform.
ROMANS 4:20-21

$\mathcal{H}$ope is grabbing the hand of God
in the fog of life and letting Him
lead you through. He will help you
be the mother you want to be.

· · · · ∾ · · · ·

As for God, His way is perfect;
the word of the LORD is proven; He is a
shield to all who trust in Him.
PSALM 18:30

*M*other always taught us that
sometimes God calms the storm—
and sometimes He calms us
in the midst of the storm.

. . . . ∾ . . . .

*Behold, the L*ORD'*s hand is not shortened,*
that it cannot save; nor His ear heavy,
that it cannot hear.
ISAIAH 59:1

The formula for being
a godly mother is simple:
You cannot do God's work,
and He will not do yours.

· · · · ∼ · · · ·

When you pass through the waters,
I will be with you; and through the rivers,
they shall not overflow you. When you walk
through the fire, you shall not be burned,
nor shall the flame scorch you.

ISAIAH 43:2

You either serve God or Satan. Neither in this life nor the next are there any "maybe" Christians.

· · · · ❧ · · · ·

The LORD is good, a stronghold in the day of trouble. And He knows those who trust in Him.

NAHUM 1:7

God has left a portrait of
Himself on the mantle of earth.
Look at a mountain, and you will
see His strength. Gaze at a flower,
and grasp His tenderness.

. . . . ≈ . . . .

I will lift up my eyes to the hills—
from whence comes my help?
PSALM 121:1

*A*lthough bats are happy in the dark, most of God's creatures need light for growth and development. As Christian mothers we need to seek God's light.

· · · · ∾ · · · ·

Let your light so shine before men,
that they may see your good works and
glorify your Father in heaven.
MATTHEW 5:16

*E*ven the humble mosquito
needs to do some serious work
before it gets a slap on the back.

. . . . ⤫ . . . .

But let each one examine his own work,
and then he will have rejoicing in himself alone,
and not in another. For each one shall bear his own load.
GALATIANS 6:4–5